D1596360

BONE APPÉTIT

For Barney and Gracie, the glee squad

BONE APPÉTIT

50 CLEAN RECIPES FOR HEALTHIER, HAPPIER DOGS

DEBORA ROBERTSON

HARPER DESIGN

An Imprint of HarperCollins Publishers

Published in 2019 by
Harper Design
An Imprint of HarperCollinsPublishers
195 Broadway
New York, NY 10007
Tel: (212) 207-7000
Fax: (855) 746-6023
harperdesign@harpercollins.com
www.hc.com

Distributed throughout North America by
HarperCollins Publishers
195 Broadway
New York, NY 10007
ISBN 978-0-06-287445-0
Library of Congress Control Number 2018961251
Printed in Singapore
Second Printing, 2021

The publisher and author are not liable for any damages
or negative consequences arising from following the
information and recipes in this book. References are
provided for informational purposes only and do not
constitute endorsement of any website, brand or other
sources. For diagnosis or treatment of any medical
problem you should always consult your own vet.

Bone Appétit

CONTENTS

The Bare Bones

Just over eleven years ago, as a clueless yet conscientious new dog owner, I ran along to a puppy class with my tiny border terrier, Barney. As we both got to grips with "Sit!" "Stay!" and "Lie down!" a high-strung woman pulled a plastic bag out of the pocket of her quilted jacket, explaining she only gave her poodle organic liver treats she'd made herself. I would have been less surprised if it had been a bag of crack. My eyes rolled so far into the back of my head I was rendered temporarily incapable of carrying out the "Look at me!" command.

Shortly afterward, my husband Séan and I took Barney to our local park and stumbled across a group of dog walkers huddled around two plastic containers of food. It was Polly the labradoodle's first birthday and there was cake for the humans and a separate cake for the dogs. I whispered to Séan, "If I ever start baking for my dog, shoot me." I'm still here. He's a very understanding man.

The truth is, I never thought I would turn into the kind of person who cooks for her dog. Now, I regularly create meals and treats for Barney, and our Dandie Dinmont puppy (look them up—the best hairdo in dogbiz), Gracie. If we're invited to a dog-owning friend's for dinner, I often tuck a box of homemade dog treats into my bag along with a bottle of red. One of the highlights of my social calendar is the dog walkers' Christmas party in our local park—mulled wine and hand pies for the humans, Doggy Breath Bones (page 70) for the hounds. Dress casual.

But I'm a feeder. If I love you, or even if I just like you a little bit, or if you're my mailman, or someone who just came to prune the wisteria, or we have just met, you're probably not leaving my house without a container filled with something good to eat.

So it's hardly surprising that if you are my dear little dogs, my constant companions, the creatures who love me despite my *Real Housewives of New York City* obsession or my capacity to eat peanut butter straight from the jar (in fact, the latter is a passion we share), then baby, pass the chopping board because I am going to express my love for you via the medium of sweet potato chews (page 79). I finally unburdened myself of my meaty little dog-cheffing secret in a piece for the *Daily Telegraph* and then a strange thing happened. I was inundated with confessional emails and tweets from readers, some eager to share recipes, all relieved to hear they weren't on their own. I was asked to write more pieces. I did lots of radio interviews. ITV's *This Morning* called to check Barney's availability. Then a magazine asked if Barney would like to review the latest gourmet dog treats. A fancy culinary school invited me to teach a class and one woman came who didn't even have a dog of her own. Then I was asked to write this book. Sometimes our careers are what happen to us while we're making other plans.

I see now that dog biscuits are the gateway snack. You begin by rustling up a tray of Peanut Butter and Banana Bites (page 72), and before you know it, you're hand-feeding your dogs Turkey and Quinoa Meatballs (page 36) as you mentally run through their menu for the week. Of course, I am aware that in a world where there are hungry humans, there is a certain Marie Antoinette-ery about feeding my dogs Chicken and Fennel au Gratin (page 60). But when you take on a pet, I think it's your responsibility to give them as happy and healthy a life as you possibly can.

As I began to feed my dogs homemade food, I quickly realized what I was doing wasn't at all complicated or expensive. In fact, my own forays into canine haute cuisine were simply an extension of how we all used to feed our dogs anyway, with scraps from the table boosted with raw bones and the odd bit of tripe from the butcher's. Those dogs of yore all seemed to live for ages, without many of the intolerances and other food-related problems we see in some dogs now.

"*My little dog —
a heartbeat at my feet.*"

Edith Wharton

I spoke to my vet, read a lot of books and papers on canine nutrition, and was conscientious about getting the balance right, but essentially what I was doing was quite simple and hugely enjoyable.

As my way of cooking for Barney and Gracie evolved, I admit there was an unexpected shift. Many of the one-pot casserole recipes I developed for my dogs, I then tweaked with extra seasonings to make them suitable for us, too (I've indicated in the following chapters each recipe where you might also want to do this). So truthfully, we now survive and thrive on the scraps from the dogs' table, and I'm here to report my coat's never been more glossy. The pack—canine and human—that eats together, stays together.

11

I do hope you'll give some of these recipes a try, whether it's simply a few biscuits from time to time or the full from-scratch experience. It's a wonderful way to build up that very special bond between you and your dog and—who knows—you may even find some recipes you enjoy yourself.

Bone appétit!

Chapter One

DOG'S PANTRY

Getting started shouldn't be daunting—you probably have many of the ingredients you need to rustle up great meals for your dog in your cupboards, refrigerator, and freezer already. That's the beauty of this method of feeding. Your dog isn't eating from cans of mystery meat and bags of dusty kibble. He's eating similar things to you, enjoying the variety and the changes in texture and flavor, just as you do.

WHAT TO EAT?

I feed my dogs about 60 percent raw and cooked meat, 20–30 percent vegetables and fruit (page 19), and 10 percent other ingredients such as eggs, healthy grains, and yogurt. Several times a week, I give them meaty bones to chew, or I will attempt to at least (see the bone about which we do not speak, page 26). If you are using the recipes from this book, try to keep these proportions in mind. If you give your dog a meal with a high vegetable or fruit content for breakfast, make sure their dinner is a meaty one.

If I'm in a hurry, or traveling, or it's just too inconvenient at that moment to make something, or to grab a meal from the freezer, I feed Barney and Gracie a good-quality prepared food—one with a high meat content where the ingredients on the label are foods I recognize and might eat myself.

For your dog to extract the most from his meal, you need to blend it in a food processor, blender, or with an immersion blender. Dogs don't chew their food like we do—their jaws move up and down, not side to side, so they can't pulp their food themselves, and there are no digestive enzymes in their saliva. Digestion starts in their stomachs, not in their mouths. If you have a dog who gobbles his food, consider food puzzle feeding bowls, which have a kind of intricate maze in the bottom so he really has to slow down and work for his supper.

DO NOT DISTURB

If your phone rings or someone comes to the door just as you're sitting down to your favorite dinner, how do you feel? Rushed, grumpy, and a bit anxious you won't enjoy your delicious meal at its best? Your dog feels the same. Never interrupt a dog while he's eating and teach other members of the household, particularly children, that they shouldn't either. It can lead to food guarding and even aggression. Always leave your dog to eat in peace.

HOW TO FEED A PUPPY

Puppies grow very quickly and you need to pay special attention to their diets in order to set them up for long, healthy lives. Their small stomachs need regular sustenance. Feed them four evenly spaced meals a day until they are four months old, then three meals a day until they are six months old, then two meals a day as you would with an adult dog.

All good breeders and many rescue centers will give you a small amount of the food they've been feeding your puppy. Gradually introduce his new diet alongside the food he's used to, starting with lightly cooked and puréed meat, fish, fruit, and vegetables, or try a high-quality commercial food specifically tailored to puppies. You can start to introduce some raw food, such as chicken wings, from around twelve weeks. Always supervise your puppy when he's chewing raw bones.

OLD FRIENDS

Older dogs require smaller, and sometimes more frequent, meals—you might want to increase the number of meals a day, if that's practical for you and desirable for him. It used to be thought that older dogs required a lower-protein diet, but there's no real evidence to back this up and any of the recipes in this book would work for your old pal. Dogs with missing teeth and sensitive mouths might enjoy their food more if it is smoothly puréed—it will help them extract maximum nutrition from it, too. The biggest issue affecting the health of many older dogs is obesity. Keep an eye on your dog's weight (page 16). He will need less food as his activity levels decrease. Gradually cut back on his food until you reach the right level and make sure what he does eat is nutritionally balanced and of high quality.

HOW MUCH TO FEED YOUR DOG?

Unlike any of the thousands of recipes I've created as a food writer, the recipes in this book don't come with a suggested number of servings. Clearly, a Chihuahua is going to eat a lot less than a Great Dane. How much food you feed your dog will depend on his breed, age, weight, and activity level.

Obesity can cause or exacerbate all kinds of problems, from diabetes and arthritis to skin problems and hip dysplasia, so pay close attention and decrease the amount of food you're feeding him if your dog begins to look a little too round. You should also be vigilant about treats, and make sure you include them as part of your dog's daily food allowance. It is very easy to forget you've given them, especially at times when you are using them regularly as training rewards, and too many of them can make the difference between a healthy weight and creeping obesity. Similarly, if your dog is underweight, he will lack stamina and be less likely to be able to fight off infection. Tailor the amount you feed him to the amount of exercise he's getting each day, too. He'll need less food on a day he's had a couple of brisk, short walks than on a day he's spent hours trekking through the countryside with you.

To get a sense of whether or not your dog is overweight, stand over your standing dog and look down at his silhouette. He should curve in at the hips and have a visible waist. Now look at him from the side. His belly should curve upwards and not hang downwards. Next, stand behind him with your palms spread out along his sides. You should be able to feel his ribs easily under his fur. Get into the habit of doing this every week or so, as it's very easy for weight to creep up or down without you noticing it immediately.

Of course, consult your vet about any unexplained or persistent weight loss or gain. For the purposes of monitoring any dietary regimen, your vet should be happy for you to drop in every week or so and use the scale at the office—so much simpler to use and more accurate than attempting to use scales you have at home.

POOP!

At the risk of sounding deranged, I am going to encourage you to pay close attention to your dog's poop. It holds so many valuable clues to his health. For a start, it will tell you what is passing through his system virtually intact (remember, blend, blend, blend, page 14).

His stools should be a rich brownish color and quite firm, but not hard. If temporarily runny, it may indicate he's having a difficult time getting used to a new food or has eaten something that doesn't agree with him (dogs can be terrible scavengers, so be vigilant about what they're picking up when you're out on walks). If his poop is copious and smells revolting, there may be too much fiber in his diet. A healthier, more balanced diet will mean smaller stools which don't smell so dreadful. I mean, obviously, they're not *delightful* on the nose, unless you're very weird, but they shouldn't make you gag. Black, tarry poop can mean bleeding high in the digestive tract; streaked with red can mean bleeding in the lower digestive tract; greyish-yellow poop can mean your dog has problems with his pancreas, liver, or gallbladder. All dogs get upset tummies from time to time, but if any unusual symptoms persist for more than a couple of days, call your vet.

Top Tips

GOOD THINGS

Fish

Fish is a good source of omega-3 fatty acids.
Fresh fish, such as salmon, should
be simply poached or roasted and you
must be very careful about removing all
bones, or use canned fish as a helpful
substitute (page 25).

Garlic

Members of the allium family such
as onions and leeks can cause anemia in
dogs and should be avoided, but small
amounts of garlic from time to time can
have beneficial bacterial, antiviral, and
antifungal properties.

Dairy

Many dogs have problems digesting milk
but can tolerate a little cheese from time
to time as a training reward, or as an
ingredient in a treat. Plain yogurt with
live active cultures is a good source of
calcium, protein, and probiotics, and can be
beneficial if served in small quantities.

Eggs

Eggs are easily digestible and a good source
of protein, amino acids, and fatty acids. Don't
toss the shells onto the compost pile—use
them to make a calcium-rich powder (page
38) to scatter over your dog's food.

Herbs

Herbs such as mint, oregano, and parsley
ensure sweet breath and help digestion.

Fruit

Fruit such as apples, ripe bananas,
blueberries, pears, and watermelon make
good snacks, or additions to meals such as
oatmeal or smoothies. Make sure
you remove the seeds from tree fruits
and melons.

Meat

Meat should provide between 60 and 75
percent of your dog's diet, but there are
other things he will enjoy and benefit from
as well. Aim for a variety of beef, chicken,
lamb, mutton, rabbit, turkey, and venison.
Include some organ meat such as liver and
kidneys, and green tripe if you can
stomach cooking it.

Vegetables

Vegetables such as broccoli, celeriac,
celery, zucchini, green beans, parsnips,
peas, pumpkin, sweet potato, and carrots.
If raw, ensure they are very well puréed.
Though dogs sometimes enjoy crunching on
carrots or pieces of broccoli, they will pass
through their digestive tracts
fairly undigested.

Top Tips

BAD THINGS

Before feeding your dog anything, make sure it's safe for him to eat. Many foods that are fine for humans can be toxic to dogs. I learned this the extremely expensive way (insure your pets, people), when Barney found his way into a Christmas dessert and had to spend three days on an IV at the vet's. Very festive.

Anything containing alcohol

Be vigilant about sauces and gravies, which often contain traces of booze.

Chocolate

Chocolate contains the stimulant theobromine, which is highly toxic to dogs.

Avocados

Avocados contain the toxin persin, which can lead to vomiting and diarrhea in some dogs.

Caffeine

Anything containing caffeine is poisonous, so keep your dog far away from your cups of coffee, tea, or energy drinks.

Cooked bones

Cooked bones can splinter and cause potentially terrible damage.

Corn on the cob

Husks can become lodged in the dog's small intestine.

Fatty leftover meat

Cut as much of the fat off as you can because too much can cause pancreatitis.

Grapes, raisins, and other vine fruits

Grapes, raisins, and other vine fruits can cause kidney failure and death, even if consumed in small amounts.

Macadamia nuts

Macadamia nuts can cause weakness, vomiting, and even depression and, like grapes and raisins, no one really knows why, so save them for your own cocktail hour.

Onions, leeks, and other alliums

Onions, leeks, and other alliums can cause gastrointestinal problems and red blood cell damage, but a little garlic from time to time can be beneficial (see page 18).

Xylitol

Peanut butter is a favorite treat for many dogs, but avoid brands containing Xylitol, a sugar substitute that is highly toxic to dogs.

Tomatoes

Nice, ripe red tomatoes are fine from time to time, but the leaves, stems, and unripe green tomatoes are potentially harmful, so pay attention when your dog is playing next to you in the garden or greenhouse.

VEGETARIAN OR VEGAN?

My thought on this is that just because you can doesn't mean you should. You may be vegetarian or vegan, which is an informed decision you have made for yourself, but your dog doesn't have the capacity to make this choice, and if you do that on his behalf, you're imposing a diet that takes him away from his natural state. Dogs' teeth, jaws, and digestive systems have evolved to eat meat, and it's the kind and respectful thing to do to give them a diet that reflects that.

KEEP IT CLEAN

When you're making your dog's dinners, it's just as important to pay attention to hygiene as it is when you make food for humans. Wash your hands before and after handling their food and make sure you use separate cutting boards for meat and vegetables. If you're batch cooking, cool dishes down quickly before refrigerating or freezing. I do this by plunging the cooling pan into a sink of cold water for casseroles; for rice and beans, I drain them and then spread them out on large platters as thinly as possible so they cool quickly. Make sure their dishes are scrupulously clean, too. When feeding them fresh food, if for any reason your dog doesn't eat it all up right away, pick it up and dispose of it after 30 minutes or so.

HOT OR COLD?

Most of the recipes in this book I serve at room temperature. I remove precooked food from the refrigerator or freezer in plenty of time to take the chill off it. Sometimes though, if one of my dogs is a little under the weather and not eating well, I warm it slightly as the increased aroma makes it more tempting to reluctant eaters.

CALCIUM QUESTION

When you're feeding your dog homemade food, it's really important to ensure he gets enough calcium. Good sources of calcium are meaty bones and eggshells (page 38), some dairy, and leafy greens, though be cautious and seek advice about feeding too many greens if your dog is prone to bladder stones.

ORGANIC OR NOT?

In an ideal world, wouldn't that be nice? But for many of us, feeding our pets a completely organic diet is an unrealistic goal. I stock up on organic meat for the dogs when I see it on sale and freeze it until I'm ready to cook it. But be reassured: By preparing your dog's food yourself, whether you use organic ingredients or not, you know exactly what's in his dinner and you are sparing him from many of the mystery ingredients in some commercial dog foods.

The Essential
DOGGY PANTRY

Brewer's yeast

Brewer's yeast in powdered form is a rich source of B vitamins, which are good for dogs' skin and coats, and may have a calming effect. It also helps deter fleas and ticks. Sprinkle a small amount over your dog's food as a condiment.

Ground flaxseeds

Ground flaxseeds are a good source of omega-3 fatty acids, which are beneficial for skin and coat, as well as a good source of dietary fiber. I buy whole flaxseeds and keep them in a sealed jar in the refrigerator, then grind them as I need them in a clean coffee grinder (make sure the grinder has no traces of coffee, as caffeine is not good for dogs).

Coconut oil

Coconut oil can help improve skin, coat, and digestion. It has antibacterial, anti-inflammatory, antiviral, and antifungal properties, but use it sparingly and don't give it to dogs prone to pancreatitis.

Rolled oats

Rolled oats are a good source of soluble fiber. Make sure you use plain, cooked oats, without any seasonings, salt, or sugar.

Millet

Millet in small amounts is a good source of beneficial minerals such as magnesium and zinc, and B vitamins. It is one of the least allergenic foods, so it's suitable for dogs who have sensitive stomachs.

Quinoa

Quinoa is high in protein and easily digestible. It's a good source of essential amino acids, minerals, vitamins, and fiber.

Rice

Rice is a good food to combine with simply poached chicken to tempt dogs who are feeling under the weather (page 102). If possible, I use brown rice which is more nutritious but bland. White rice is more digestible for very sickly dogs.

Canned fish

Canned fish such as salmon, sardines, and tuna makes the basis of great impromptu meals (pages 39, 46, and 62).

RAW FEEDING

In recent years, raw feeding has become increasingly popular among dog owners, inspired by the seminal book *Give Your Dog a Bone* by Australian vet Ian Billinghurst. The BARF diet (Biologically Appropriate Raw Feeding, or Bones And Raw Food) works on the principle that dogs' digestive systems are designed to process raw meat and bones as well as small amounts of vegetables and fruit. Their stomachs are much more acidic than ours and so are entirely capable of breaking down raw flesh and bone.

You can create this diet yourself. There are many excellent books and online sources to guide you, and certainly consult your vet and/or a canine nutritionist to get you started. Get the bones and inexpensive but high-quality scraps of meat from your butcher. If you have a big freezer, you can buy lots of meaty bones at once which is a great time-saver; freezing can also help destroy any harmful surface bacteria.

Alternatively, use one of the many companies that will do it all for you, providing a wide range of products where the bone, meat, and vegetables are ground up together and frozen. All you need to do is defrost and serve.

Whether you follow the BARF program or not, it's a good idea to give your dog some tasty, meaty, raw bones at least a couple of times a week as part of his regular diet. Chewing takes up energy and releases endorphins, the happy hormone, so not only do bones help your dog keep his teeth clean and jaw strong, they help make him calm and cheerful, too.

It's true that some dogs never take to eating bones. Barney's interest in meaty bones extends to burying them in the garden and then waiting patiently for weeks until they achieve the perfect level of revoltingness before gleefully reappearing with them in the house. And then there was the bone about which we do not speak. A rather grand woman came to measure a sofa that needed reupholstering. As she removed the cushions, she gingerly produced between her manicured fingers an ancient lamb leg bone. "I think this belongs to him," she said, witheringly. She seemed the type who would disapprove of animals being allowed on the furniture at all, let alone burying their dinner down the back of it. Oh well... you can't say I didn't try.

WHAT A TREAT!

Treats should always be included in your dog's daily food allowance and should form only about 10 percent of his diet at the absolute most. Smelly foods, such as liver treats, scraps of cheese, or tiny bits of hot dog, make good training rewards, but you should keep your dog guessing and change the treat frequently so he's never sure what he's going to get. Don't forget, food is not the only treat—attention from you, games, or being allowed to do something he really loves can be just as motivating to your dog as food.

Chapter Two

EVERYDAY EATING

This chapter contains some of the
building blocks of a lucky pup's day-to-day diet, from
easy-to-digest breakfast smoothies and oatmeal, to
homemade kibble, meaty stocks, and easily assembled
suppers, such as fishcakes and omelettes. All of these
dishes are inexpensive and simple to prepare, and—
a bonus—like many of the recipes in this book, quite
a few of them can be tweaked to make them just as
delicious for you as they are for your dog.

BANANA SMOOTHIE

🐾 1 small banana or half a large banana
🐾 ½ cup (100 ml) plain yogurt
🐾 ½ tsp honey

 Tip You can freeze this in ice cube trays as a treat for a hot day (page 94).

REMEMBER

How much you feed your dog depends on her size, weight, and the amount of exercise she is getting. See page 16 for more details.

Makes
1
large smoothie

Smoothies are not just for when your dog's having a Gwyneth Paltrow moment. Bananas are a great source of fiber, which helps treat mild bouts of constipation or diarrhea, and potassium, which is important for both muscle and blood vessel function. Make sure the banana is ripe, because green bananas are hard for dogs to digest. I don't add milk because lots of dogs have problems digesting lactose, but if you would like to thin it down a bit, mix in some water, oat milk, goat milk, or coconut water.

1. Blend the ingredients together in a blender or mash together with a fork until smooth.

VARIATION

Add a few blueberries or strawberries, or a teaspoon of salt and Xylitol-free peanut butter (page 21).

PUPPY OATMEAL

🐾 6 tbsp (50 g) rolled oats

🐾 1 ½ cups (350 ml) water

🐾 3 ½ tbsp (50 ml) coconut milk, goat milk, or plain yogurt (optional)

Other additions

- A handful of blueberries—I always save some of these from the oatmeal for my puppy Gracie, who loves to chase them around the kitchen floor in a happy breakfast forage.

- Some chopped, ripe banana
- A little grated apple
- ½ tsp honey
- Pinch of ground cinnamon

Makes

1

large bowl

This is not just for young hounds, but is a great occasional breakfast for all dogs, large and small. Oats are a good source of soluble fiber, and can help soothe skin complaints and aid troubled digestion. Make sure you choose plain, rolled oats—some quick-cook brands can contain salt, sugar, and other no-nos such as artificial sweeteners—and adjust the serving size to suit your dog.

1. Put the oats and water into a small nonstick saucepan and warm over medium heat, stirring, for about 6–7 minutes (or follow the package instructions) until cooked thoroughly. Remove from the heat and stir in the milk or yogurt, if using. Cool to room temperature before stirring in the fruit or other flavorings. You can make this the night before if you like. It keeps in the refrigerator for a couple of days, or you can freeze it in serving-sized portions for up to 3 months.

VARIATIONS

- You can make this with half oats and half quinoa, which is a good source of protein. Rinse the quinoa well before simmering for 15 minutes. Add the oats after about 8 minutes.
- Oatmeal—either plain or mixed with quinoa—is a great vehicle for other ingredients, especially leftovers. Add chopped-up cooked meat and vegetables such as carrots, green beans, pumpkin, or sweet potato. You can also simmer raw, ground meat in the oatmeal until it's cooked thoroughly.

FOR HUMANS

If you're making this for humans, add a little salt and some sugar, maple syrup, or honey.

STOCKS OF
ALL KINDS

Slowly simmered stock is intensely nutritious and great for sick or recovering dogs, or simply as an addition to their normal food. This recipe is based on the recipe for bone broth by my friends and fellow dog lovers Jasmine and Melissa Hemsley, though obviously it omits leeks and onions. If you don't have any vegetables or herbs on hand, you can simply simmer the bones with vinegar or lemon juice. The added bonus: You can use this as an ingredient in all of your own soups and casseroles, too.

- 🐾 4 lb 8 oz–6 lb 8 oz (2–3 kg) beef bones, lamb bones, or turkey or chicken carcasses; you can also add some chicken wings or scraps of leftover meat or meat trimmings if you like, or use a combination of raw and cooked bones
- 🐾 2–4 carrots, scrubbed and roughly chopped
- 🐾 2–3 celery ribs, roughly chopped, plus celery tops, too, if you have them
- 🐾 1 bunch of parsley, stalks and leaves, roughly chopped
- 🐾 2 tbsp cider vinegar or the freshly squeezed juice of a lemon, to help extract the minerals from the bones

Makes

1

large pot

1. Place all ingredients in a large stockpot and pour in enough cold water to cover by 2 in (5 cm). Bring to a boil, skim off any foam that rises to the surface, then cover and simmer very gently for longer than you would ever think possible. Chicken bones should be crumbly, and more substantial bones should be bleached white. Essentially, you need to simmer them very gently, covered, for 8–24 hours—beef bones need the longest simmering time. Keep an eye on the pan and give it a good stir every few hours. Top up with water from time to time. You can also cook stock very well in a pressure cooker or slow cooker (page 64).

2. Place a fine sieve over a large bowl or pan and strain the stock. Cool rapidly by placing the bowl in a sink of iced water. Sealed in a container, the stock will keep in the refrigerator for 5 days, or in the freezer for 4 months. You can also freeze the stock in ice cube trays for a hot-day treat, or so that you have enough for handy single servings to moisten other meals.

VARIATIONS

- Fish stock is also a great addition to your dog's diet. Most fishmongers will give you fish bones and heads for free. Make it exactly as above and simmer for 8 hours.
- You can make a nutritious and tasty broth simply with well-scrubbed vegetable peelings and trimmings (remember, no onions or leeks). Cram them into a pan, cover with water, and simmer for an hour or two.

TURKEY AND
QUINOA MEATBALLS

- 🐾 1 lb 2 oz (500 g) ground turkey or chicken
- 🐾 1 ¼ cups (200 g) black, red, or golden quinoa, cooked amount [approximately ⅓ cup (60 g) uncooked]
- 🐾 7 oz (200 g) fresh spinach, lightly cooked, chopped, drained, and patted dry

- 🐾 2 tbsp ground flaxseeds (optional)
- 🐾 1 tsp freshly chopped rosemary (optional)

For the optional dipping sauce

- 🐾 A few tablespoons of plain yogurt, mixed with a little bit of finely chopped mint

Makes
35
approx.

Quinoa is a great source of protein, and combined with the turkey or chicken, it makes a tasty and easily digestible snack. Of course, you can use ground beef or lamb if you prefer. Add the yogurt dipping sauce if you want to be extra fancy. Which, of course, you do.

• •

1. Preheat the oven to 400°F. Line a roasting pan with baking parchment.

2. Mix all the ingredients together in a bowl until well combined. Roll into walnut-sized meatballs (you should be able to make about 35). Place them on the lined pan and bake in the preheated oven for 25 minutes until cooked thoroughly and lightly browned. Cool before feeding them to your dog, with a dollop of the yogurt dipping sauce if you like.

3. The meatballs will keep in the refrigerator for a couple of days or you can freeze them for up to 4 months.

FOR
HUMANS

If you're making these for humans, season them well with salt and pepper, break off a small piece and fry until cooked thoroughly and taste. Adjust seasoning if necessary and then either bake as above or fry until cooked thoroughly in a little olive oil.

OMELETTES

Eggs are a great source of protein and are easily digestible. Make sure you cook them through completely because uncooked egg whites can lead to a biotin deficiency in dogs which adversely affects their skin and coats—admittedly, they would have to eat a lot of egg whites, but why take the risk? Sometimes, if I have an abundance of egg whites left over from making ice cream or custard with the yolks, I make Barney and Gracie egg white omelettes for supper—there's only so many meringues a person needs, after all.

- ¼ tsp olive oil
- 2 eggs, lightly beaten

Other additions

- Add a couple of spoonfuls of cottage cheese to the cooked omelette before rolling it up.
- Stir in some scraps of cooked meat or fish just before the omelette sets.
- Cooked, finely chopped broccoli, green beans, and/or kale are a good addition.

1. Warm the oil in a small, nonstick frying pan over medium-high heat. Pour in the eggs and, as they begin to set, tilt the pan and lift up the edges of the omelette with a spatula, allowing the uncooked egg to run around the sides. Once set, slide onto a plate and cool.

2. If your dog doesn't eat it all, leftover omelettes will keep covered in the refrigerator for a day.

Tip

Eggshell powder

Eggshells are a good source of calcium. Many dogs will happily chew on the shells as they are, but if you are worried about the sharp edges, just dry them in a low oven and blend them into a powder in a food processor, blender, or coffee grinder. I keep the powder in a jam jar and simply sprinkle it over Barney and Gracie's food.

Makes

1

omelette

SALMON FISHCAKES

I always have some cans of salmon in the cupboard, because they make a good, quick, healthy lunch for humans and dogs alike. Salmon is a great source of omega-3 fatty acids and protein. You can make this with fresh salmon if you like, but make sure you cook it first—raw salmon can contain a parasite that is harmful to dogs.

- 6–7 oz (170–200 g) canned salmon, drained if necessary
- 1 hard-boiled egg, finely chopped
- ½ cup (100 g) cooked mashed potato or mashed sweet potato
- ⅓ cup (50 g) peas, cooked, or a combination of peas and cooked, finely diced carrots
- 2 tbsp finely chopped parsley

1. Mix all the ingredients together well and form into round cakes. Serve them as they are, or bake them at 350°F for 18–20 minutes until cooked thoroughly and firm, to create a more portable meal.

2. They will keep in the refrigerator for a couple of days, cooked or uncooked, or in the freezer for up to 4 months.

39

VARIATION

You can use canned tuna or sardines instead of salmon if you like.

FOR HUMANS

If making these for humans, add some salt, perhaps some chopped chilis and scallions, and serve with a Thai dipping sauce. Or dip them in a little beaten egg, coat them in fine breadcrumbs, and fry until golden and cooked thoroughly, turning once, about 8–10 minutes. Children in particular seem to enjoy them cooked like this.

HOMEMADE KIBBLE

A good, crunchy meal without any of the mystery ingredients so prevalent in commercial versions. This is great to take with you when you're traveling, too.

- ❧ A little oil, for greasing
- ❧ About 9 oz (250 g) cooked meat (I often make this on Mondays, using the leftovers from Sunday's roast chicken, lamb, or beef)
- ❧ About ¾ cup (125 g) cooked vegetables, such as carrots, butternut squash, or sweet potatoes (often left over from Sunday's roast dinner, too—as long as they aren't too oily or heavily seasoned with salt)
- ❧ 2 tsp ground flaxseeds (optional)
- ❧ About ¾ cup (100 g) buckwheat flour or brown rice flour, plus a little more for dusting

Other additions

- · Add a few tablespoons of rolled oats if you like.
- · Throw in some chicken livers, too.
- · A sprinkling of eggshell powder (page 38) is a good addition.

Tip   Once I have baked this in the oven, I sometimes finish it off with a few hours in my dehydrator (pages 78-9), to make sure it's absolutely bone dry, which prolongs how long it can be kept.

Makes
1
large jar

1. Preheat the oven to 285°F. Lightly grease a couple of baking pans.

2. Blend together the meat and vegetables in a food processor, along with the flaxseeds if using, until smooth. Add the flour a few tablespoons at a time, just until you have a fairly stiff dough.

3. Turn out the dough onto a sheet of baking parchment lightly dusted with flour, knead into a flattish ball, and roll out until ¼ in (5 mm) thick. Cut to the same size as your baking pan and turn onto your prepared pan, peeling off the parchment. Score the dough into bite-sized squares with a knife, cutting all the way through. Roll out any scraps of dough to make more kibble, too.

4. Bake in the preheated oven for 1 hour. Turn off the heat and leave the kibble in the cooling oven for a few hours to dry out. You want to make sure it's absolutely dried out or it will go moldy within a few days. It will keep in an airtight container for a week, or you can freeze it for up to 4 months.

MEATLOAF

Always a delicious lunchtime favorite, why deprive your dog of the
pleasure? You can make this in two large batches and bake one batch
for your dog, and another seasoned batch for yourself. Use either
an 8x4-inch loaf pan, a 12-hole muffin tin, or a 24-hole mini-muffin tin.

- 🐾 A little olive oil, for greasing
- 🐾 1 lb 10 oz (750 g) ground beef
- 🐾 1¼ cups (250 g) prepared vegetables—choose from a
  mixture of puréed, cooked carrot, potato, sweet potato and/
  or butternut squash; cooked, chopped green beans, peas,
  kale, or cabbage; grated zucchini or apple
- 🐾 1 egg, lightly beaten
- 🐾 3–4 tbsp finely chopped parsley, stalks and all
- 🐾 1 tsp finely chopped rosemary
- 🐾 1 tsp ground flaxseeds (optional)
- 🐾 A little salt-free tomato paste (optional)

Makes
1
large loaf

1. Preheat the oven to 400°F. Brush the loaf or muffin tin lightly with olive oil.

2. In a bowl, mix together all of the ingredients—apart from the tomato paste—until very well combined. Press into the prepared pan or tin and smear a tiny bit of tomato paste over the top of the mixture if you like. Place the pan or tin on a baking sheet and bake a large meatloaf for 50 minutes, small meatloaves for 25–30 minutes, and 20 minutes for mini muffins, until cooked thoroughly. Cool in the pans before removing.

3. Cut the larger meatloaf into slices. Freeze any slices or individual loaves you don't use immediately for up to 4 months.

VARIATIONS

- You can also use ground turkey, or a mixture of ground venison and beef.
- You can also add a little leftover Puppy Oatmeal (page 32) if you like.
- Stir in some raw chicken livers if you have them.
- Use the same mixture to make burgers if you prefer.

Love your
LEFTOVERS

Just as we humans often find the prospect of leftovers to be the most enticing part of a meal, so there is much to delight our dogs in the unexpected pleasures of the remains of yesterday's dinner. In my own cooking, I often create "planned-overs," so the labor of creating one meal can create the foundations for several. It's just as easy to roast two chickens as one, or to cook twice as much brown rice or quinoa, or to steam more servings of vegetables than you need for one meal. Cooking this way ensures you have near-instant, healthy foundations for your own meals as well as your dog's.

Of course, there are certain guidelines to follow. Avoid any of the obviously toxic foods (pages 20–1), but also make sure that ostensibly healthy foods are prepared in a suitable way—no complex, salty sauces enriched with wine and onions, for example, and cut out any excess fat. Many vets report an increase in the cases of pancreatitis they see in dogs after the holiday season, when otherwise healthy hounds are often fed excessively rich foods.

With all of this in mind, here are some of the simply prepared foods your dog might like. Start small, introducing new ingredients slowly and in modest portions until you know your dog enjoys them and can digest them happily. With leftovers, it is even more important to observe the basic hygiene rules outlined on page 22.

Cooked meat

Chicken, turkey, game birds, beef, lamb, rabbit, venison; be sure to remove any bones.

Cooked fish

Be sure to remove any bones.

Cooked vegetables

Broccoli, cabbage, carrots, cauliflower, zucchini, kale, green beans, parsnips, peas, pumpkin, spinach, squash, sweet potato; all prepared without too much fat or salt.

Stock or broth

A few spoonfuls.

Cooked grains

Brown rice, lentils, millet, oats, pearl barley, quinoa, spelt.

Scraps of cheese

A few scraps of grated cheese or the scrapings from a carton of cottage cheese.

The ends of a carton of plain yogurt

This is a good game, actually. Both my dogs love licking out what is left in the carton and chasing it around the kitchen with the ends of their noses. Keep an eye on them, though—the temptation to eat the carton as well is strong.

USE WHAT YOU HAVE

We all have those days when we have to fix dinner in a rush, for the human and canine members of our families. Here are some of the healthy, easy dishes I reach for when I want to feed my dogs quickly and well. They rely on canned fish, which I always have in the cupboard, combined with almost any cooked vegetables, and sometimes cooked eggs or grains such as rice and barley.

- A can of tuna mixed with cooked potato

- A can of sardines mixed with brown rice and peas

- Scrambled eggs mixed with a can of salmon

- Cooked quinoa mixed with canned mackerel and cooked spinach or broccoli

- Plain, cooked chicken with diced, cooked pumpkin, squash, or sweet potato

MANNERS MAKETH
THE MUTT

I'm a pretty free and easygoing person, but good table manners
matter enormously to me, whether they're of the human or canine
variety. If you are feeding your dog leftovers, do her the courtesy of
serving them in her own bowl. Never feed dogs from the table, unless
you wish to spend every mealtime with your dog's eyes trained on you
in the manner of an assassin waiting for the perfect moment. Begging
is a difficult habit to break, so don't let it take hold.

Chapter Three

ONE-POT DINNERS

The appeal of one-pot cooking is that it's simple, frugal, and quick—in the preparation, anyway. It's enormously forgiving and almost infinitely adaptable. No butternut squash? Use sweet potato. No lamb? Use beef instead. It also cuts down on the cleanup—always a good thing.

BEEF, BARLEY, AND BROCCOLI CASSEROLE

I created this recipe not just because I like the alliteration, but because barley is high in fiber and very easily digestible, so it makes a good addition to your repertoire of recipes for your dog. Tasty, ripe, cooked tomatoes are a good source of lycopene, a beneficial antioxidant, too.

- ½ tsp olive oil
- 1 lb 5 oz (600 g) stewing beef
- 2 diced carrots, scrubbed and cut into ¼ in (5 mm) pieces
- 1 celery rib, diced into ¼ in (5 mm) pieces (if you have leaves, chop them finely and add them at the end)
- 14 oz (400 g) canned chopped tomatoes
- 1⅔ cups (400 ml) homemade stock (page 34) or water
- ½ cup (80 g) pearl barley, rinsed
- 6 oz (175 g) broccoli, roughly chopped into small pieces
- 2 tbsp finely chopped parsley or oregano, leaves and stems

 Tip

If you don't have any stock, you can use the water you cooked the vegetables in, as long as they haven't been cooked with salt.

REMEMBER

How much you feed your dog depends on his size, weight, and the amount of exercise he is getting. See page 16 for more details.

Makes
1
large pot

1. Warm the oil in a heavy saucepan over medium heat and add the beef, carrots, and celery and cook, stirring for 5 minutes. Add in the tomatoes and stock or water and bring to a simmer. Add the barley, return to a simmer, lower the heat, cover, and cook for 1 hour, until the beef is tender and the barley is cooked thoroughly. Add the broccoli and cook for another 10 minutes. Remove from the heat, stir in the herbs and any celery tops you might have. Cool before serving.

2. If you like, cook this in a slow cooker for around 8 hours, or in a pressure cooker on high for 25–30 minutes.

3. It will keep sealed in the refrigerator for 3–4 days, or in the freezer for 4 months.

FOR HUMANS

If you want to serve this to humans, remove the portion for your dog and season what remains with salt and pepper, and possibly a generous dash of Worcestershire sauce. Serve with buttery mashed potatoes.

LAMB, MILLET, AND SQUASH STEW

- ½ tsp olive oil
- 1 lb 2 oz (500 g) stewing lamb
- 1 garlic clove, finely chopped (optional)
- 2 ¼ cups (500 ml) stock (page 34) or water
- Scant ½ cup (80 g) millet

- 10 ½ oz (300 g) butternut squash, peeled, deseeded, and diced into ½ in (1 cm) pieces
- ⅔ cup (100 g) peas, fresh or frozen
- 2 tbsp finely chopped mint

Tip You can use leftover roast lamb cut into cubes or ground lamb if you like.

Makes
1
large pot

Lamb can be a good source of protein for dogs who show a sensitivity to other meats such as beef or chicken. Millet is also one of the least allergenic foods, so together with the easily digestible squash, this makes a soothing and nutritious meal.

• •

1. Warm the oil in a heavy saucepan over medium-high heat and add the lamb. Cook, stirring from time to time, for 5 minutes. Lower the heat, add the garlic if using, and stir for a minute. Pour in the stock, bring to a simmer, cover, and cook for 30 minutes. Add the millet and squash and cook for another 30 minutes, stirring from time to time, until the meat is very tender. Add the peas, cook for 5 minutes more, remove from the heat, and stir in the mint. Cool before serving.

2. If you like, cook this in a slow cooker for around 8 hours, or in a pressure cooker on high for 25–30 minutes.

3. It will keep sealed in the refrigerator for 3–4 days, or in the freezer for 4 months.

FOR HUMANS

If you want to serve this to humans, remove the portion for your dog and season what remains with salt and pepper, and more mint and/or some parsley. It's good hot or cold.

BEEF HASH WITH CABBAGE AND POTATOES

This is a great, delicious recipe which is very quick to make. As with so many dishes, it can be improved—and the protein content increased—with the addition of an egg. When you spoon the hash into your dog's bowl, simply top with a cooled, boiled, or poached egg.

- ½ tsp olive oil
- About 10½ oz (300 g) leftover roast beef, cut into ½–¾ in (1–2 cm) chunks
- 2 small (about 7 oz/200 g) potatoes, unpeeled, scrubbed, and diced into ½ in (1 cm) pieces
- 3½ oz (100 g) cabbage, finely shredded
- 1¾ cups (400 ml) stock (page 34) or water
- 1 tsp finely chopped rosemary (optional)

1. Warm the olive oil in a large frying pan over medium-high heat. Add the beef, potatoes, and cabbage, stir, then pour in the stock and add the rosemary, if using. Simmer with the lid on, stirring from time to time, until the potatoes and cabbage are very tender, about 15–20 minutes.

2. This will keep sealed in the refrigerator for 3–4 days, or in the freezer for 4 months.

FOR HUMANS

If you'd like to try this for your human supper, season well and add a good splash of Worcestershire sauce before topping with an egg.

VARIATION

This is a delicious way to use up leftover roast lamb, too.

Makes

1

large pot

CHICKEN, LENTIL, AND KALE STEW

This is so quick to prepare and very tasty. I prefer to use chicken thighs because they're relatively inexpensive and full of flavor. You can certainly cook them with the bone in if you prefer—just be very careful to remove every last piece of bone before serving.

- 1 lb 2 oz (500 g) skinless, boneless chicken thighs, cut into small chunks
- 2 ¼ cups (500 ml) stock (page 34) or water
- ½ cup (100 g) green lentils, well rinsed
- 3 ½ oz (100 g) kale, very finely shredded, about 2 ½ cups
- 1 garlic clove, finely chopped (optional)
- 1 tsp finely chopped rosemary

1. Combine all the ingredients in a heavy saucepan or casserole. Bring to a simmer, stir, lower the temperature, cover with a lid and cook very gently until everything is very tender, about 35 minutes. Cool before serving, and don't forget to remove any bones if you left them in.

2. It will keep sealed in the refrigerator for 3–4 days, or in the freezer for 4 months.

 Tip Lentils are a good source of protein and fiber and are highly digestible. I use green lentils here, but you can certainly use red ones, which don't hold their shape so well and will make a creamier, softer stew. I love lentils and often combine them with brown rice in dishes for Barney and Gracie.

BRAISED BEEF CHEEKS

with carrots and green beans

- 🐾 1 tsp olive oil
- 🐾 1 large carrot, scrubbed and finely diced
- 🐾 1 large parsnip, scrubbed and finely diced
- 🐾 1 small celeriac, peeled and finely diced
- 🐾 1 celery rib, finely diced
- 🐾 3–4 sprigs of fresh thyme
- 🐾 2 beef cheeks, about 1 lb 12 oz (800 g)

- 🐾 2 ¼ cups (500 ml) stock (page 34) or water
- 🐾 14 oz (400 g) canned chopped tomatoes
- 🐾 5 ½ oz (150 g) green beans, trimmed and sliced into ½ in (1 cm) pieces
- 🐾 1 apple, cored and grated
- 🐾 4–5 tbsp freshly chopped parsley, stems and leaves

Tip

To make this recipe in a slow cooker, cook on low for 8 hours, adding the green beans and apple during the last 30 minutes. For pressure cookers, cook on high pressure for 35–40 minutes. Release the pressure, add the green beans and apples, and cook for another 5 minutes on high pressure.

Makes

1

large pot

Until relatively recently, cuts of beef such as cheeks or shin were often overlooked, but now they are the favorites of thrifty chefs everywhere because they are packed with flavor and inexpensive when compared to other cuts. Your dog will definitely appreciate this gastropub-style dinner.

1. Warm the olive oil in a heavy saucepan or casserole over medium heat. Add the carrot, parsnip, celeriac, celery, and thyme and cook, stirring, for 5 minutes. Add the beef cheeks and cook, turning once, for 5 minutes. Pour in the stock and tomatoes, bring to a simmer, reduce the heat, and cover. Cook very gently for about 4 hours until the beef is tender and falling apart—check from time to time to make sure it isn't drying out. Add more stock or water if necessary.

2. When the beef is cooked, add the beans and apple and cook for another 5–10 minutes, then add the parsley. Shred the meat and cool before serving.

3. This makes quite a lot, and it will keep sealed in the refrigerator for 3–4 days, or you can store it in individual portions in the freezer for 4 months.

FOR HUMANS

If you'd like to try this for your human supper, remove the portion for your dog and season what remains with salt and pepper, and perhaps stir in a generous spoonful of horseradish to add a little fire. A few herby dumplings wouldn't be amiss either.

SHEPHERD'S PIE WITH SWEET POTATO MASH

I'm making this with ground lamb here, but of course you can make
it in the traditional fashion with leftover roast lamb if you prefer.
Or use ground beef for a cottage pie, or ground pork for a pigpen
pie (I made that last one up).

For the lamb

* ½ tsp olive oil
* 2 carrots, scrubbed and diced into ¼ in (5 mm) pieces
* 1 celery rib, finely diced
* 1 garlic clove, finely chopped
* 1 lb 2 oz (500 g) ground lamb
* 1 scant cup (200 ml) goat milk
* 14 oz (400 g) canned chopped tomatoes
* 400 ml/14 fl oz chicken, lamb, or beef stock (page 34) or water
* 1 tsp finely chopped rosemary
* 1½ cups (150 g) peas, fresh or frozen

For the mash

* 2 lb 4 oz (1 kg) sweet potatoes, peeled and cut into 1¼ in
  (3 cm) chunks
* 1 tsp olive oil

 Tip   Make extra lamb and mash and freeze it in ice cube trays to add
instant deliciousness to other meals.

Makes
1
large pie

1. For the lamb, warm the oil in a heavy saucepan or casserole over medium heat. Add the carrots and celery and stir until softened, about 5 minutes. Add the garlic and stir for a minute. Turn up the heat a bit and add the lamb, breaking it up with a fork. Cook, stirring, until the meat is browned, about 10 minutes.

2. Pour in the milk and simmer, stirring from time to time, until the milk has almost evaporated, then add in the tomatoes, stock or water, and rosemary. Simmer for 1 hour, stirring from time to time and topping up with a splash of water if it looks dry, until you have a rich, meaty sauce. Add the peas, cook for a minute or two, then remove from the heat.

3. While the lamb is cooking, make the mashed potatoes. Add the sweet potatoes into a pan with enough water to cover. Bring to a simmer and cook until the sweet potatoes are tender, about 15–20 minutes. Drain and mash with the olive oil.

59

4. Spoon some cooled lamb into your dog's bowl with some cooled mashed sweet potatoes. Any leftovers will keep covered in the refrigerator for 3–4 days, or in the freezer for up to 4 months.

FOR
HUMANS

If you are making this for your human supper, preheat the oven to 400°F. Season the remaining ground meat well with salt, pepper, and Worcestershire sauce, then add to an ovenproof dish. Season the sweet potatoes and spread over the top. Sprinkle some grated cheese on top if you like. Bake until bubbling, about 25 minutes.

CHICKEN AND FENNEL AU GRATIN

This is a rather sophisticated supper for the dog about town. Fennel is full of antioxidants and good for digestion, and sage helps promote sweet breath. The crumbs sprinkled over the top add an appealing crunch, but do leave them out if you can't be bothered—your dog probably won't hold it against you too much.

- ½ tsp olive oil
- 1 fennel bulb, halved, cored, and very finely shredded
- 1 celery rib, finely diced
- 1 carrot, scrubbed and diced into ¼ in (5 mm) pieces
- 1 garlic clove, finely chopped (optional)
- 1 tsp buckwheat flour or brown rice flour
- 2 ½ cups (600 ml) chicken or vegetable stock (page 34), or water
- 4 skinless chicken thighs (You can cook them with the bone in if you like, though make sure you remove every trace of bone once cooked)
- 4–6 fresh sage leaves, shredded
- 2 Doggy Breath Bones (page 70) or other dog biscuits
- Grated Parmesan cheese (optional)

Tip You can add a tablespoon or two of pearl barley to this if you like. Simmer it in the broth for 30 minutes.

Makes
1
large dish

1. Warm the oil in a casserole or heavy saucepan over medium heat. Sauté the fennel, stirring from time to time, until softened, about 10 minutes. Add the celery, carrot, and garlic and sauté for a minute, then sprinkle on the flour and stir it in with the vegetables for 2–3 minutes until everything is well coated. Add the stock or water and bring to a simmer, then add the chicken thighs. Cook the chicken for 15 minutes until it's cooked thoroughly, then scoop the meat out with a slotted spoon and leave to cool.

2. Preheat the oven to 400°F.

3. Simmer the broth until it is very thick and creamy. Remove the bones from the chicken if necessary, then shred the chicken into small pieces and return to the broth. Stir in the sage, then pour into an ovenproof dish. With a pestle and mortar or food processor, grind the biscuits into crumbs and sprinkle them over the top. Add the cheese if using, then bake in the preheated oven until the top is crisp, about 15–20 minutes. Cool to room temperature before serving.

4. Any leftovers will keep covered in the refrigerator for 3–4 days, or in the freezer for up to 4 months.

FOR HUMANS

If you're making this for your human supper, season well and skip the dog biscuits—add a scattering of breadcrumbs instead.

SARDINE AND
SWEET POTATO BAKE

Sardines are so delicious, nutritious, and—a great doggy bonus—
smelly. This is a very easy dish and, because it stinks a bit, it's a
great vehicle for hiding medication for pill-averse hounds.

- 🐾 8½ oz (240 g) canned sardines in olive oil
- 🐾 1 small sweet potato, about 9 oz (250 g), scrubbed and
  very thinly sliced with a mandolin or sharp knife
- 🐾 Leaves from a few sprigs of fresh thyme

Tip

If you're in a hurry and you have some leftover cooked sweet
potato or ordinary potatoes, simply mix them up with some
canned sardines and any other cooked vegetables such as peas,
green beans, and carrots. This is one of Barney and Gracie's
favorite Sunday night snacks.

Makes
1
large dish

1. Preheat the oven to 400°F.

2. Drain the oil from the sardines into a bowl. Toss the sweet potato slices and thyme in the oil until well coated. Line an ovenproof dish with half the slices. Mash the sardines roughly with a fork and spread them over the sweet potato slices, then top with the remaining slices. Cover tightly with foil and bake until the sweet potato is very tender when pierced with the point of a sharp knife, about 45 minutes. Cool a bit before serving.

VARIATION

You can also make this recipe with canned salmon. Simply toss the sweet potato slices in a little olive oil before layering them up.

FOR HUMANS

This is quite delicious just as it is, if you would like to serve it for your human companions. Remove the foil for the last 10 minutes to let the top crisp up a bit and serve with a green salad.

QUICK, QUICK, SLOW

I used to be terrified of using a pressure cooker, but then my friend, food writer Catherine Phipps, wrote such an inspiring book* about cooking with this misunderstood piece of kitchen equipment. I couldn't resist giving one a try and now I'm hooked. A pressure cooker reduces the toughest cuts of meat to melting tenderness in less than an hour and is a terrific asset if, like me, you're often in a rush. Others prefer the low-pressure charms of the slow cooker. They allow you to throw all the ingredients into the pot before you go to work and then come home to the delicious aroma of simmering goodness eight or so hours later.

They are both useful kitchen appliances, whether you are cooking for the human or canine members of your family, and which one you choose is entirely up to your temperament. They are great for rustling up homemade dog food, from batches of nutritious stock to full, meaty meals.

As a guideline, if you're using a pressure cooker to make stock (page 34), bring it to a boil, skim off any foam, put the lid on, and cook at high pressure for an hour. If you're using a slow cooker, cook on high for 12 hours, or even longer if you have time. For meaty meals, most combinations will cook in a pressure cooker in about 25 minutes, or in a slow cooker in about 8 hours.

> * It's called—surprise, surprise—*The Pressure Cooker Cookbook: Over 150 Simple, Essential, Time-saving Recipes.* You should probably get it if you're impatient, like me.

PLANNING AHEAD

I know you're busy. I am going to try to make it as easy as possible for you to feed your dog healthy, homemade food without adding even more chores to your to-do list. I know that if this isn't easy and, I hope, fun, you're probably not going to stick with it. I know this because I wouldn't either. Here are the techniques I've developed to make this possible, hell, even enjoyable, in my own busy, easily distractible, too-much-to-do life.

I freeze cooked rice, grains, and beans in large ice cube trays to add to simple meals.

Most of the soupy, stewy recipes can be doubled, tripled, or quadrupled without much difficulty. Simply freeze them in portion sizes for up to four months (possibly longer, though they will stay in their optimum state for this long).

When I'm steaming vegetables, I often make more than I need and freeze what we don't eat in small portions so I can use them to create near-instant meals with the addition of a can of fish or some leftover cooked meat.

Stocks (page 34), again frozen in ice cube trays, add instant flavor to quick dinners.

Pack Lunch

The pack that eats together—whether that pack be human, canine, or a mixture of the two—stays together. There is something enormously satisfying about feeding your beloved dog food that you would cheerfully eat yourself. They do so much for our happiness and well-being that it seems a relatively small thing to return the favor with a few tasty dinners and the odd handful of homemade biscuits.

One of the thoughts I had when I began to work on this book was that it would be a good idea to make as many of the recipes as possible devourable by humans as well as dogs, with only the smallest of tweaks. In part, I wanted to do this because it's time efficient, but also because—I admit it—I like the idea of sitting down to a plate of chicken and fennel au gratin, as my dogs dive enthusiastically into bowls of the same thing.

So for the most part, the recipes you find here will work for all the members of your family. I avoided all of the obviously unsuitable ingredients (pages 20-1) and focused on what would work for both species. The biggest challenge was giving up onions and salt, and using garlic only very sparingly, but it was fun, and no one starved (the dogs) or died of boredom (me).

For many of the recipes, I give suggestions for how you might adapt the recipe to please your human family, but as a rule of thumb:

Complete the recipe, put to one side the portion you would like to serve to your dog, then season what remains to your own taste. Be generous with salt, pepper, chilis and other spices, handfuls of freshly chopped herbs, and condiments such as Worcestershire sauce, Tabasco sauce, and mustard.

For some of the more stewy dishes, a few dumplings bobbing on the surface, or a savory crumble or cobbler topping, or a pastry lid make for a very substantial meal.

Add a handful of grated cheese and pop the finished dish under a preheated broiler until golden and bubbling.

For sweeter dishes such as smoothies and oatmeal, add honey or maple syrup to taste. For biscuits such as the Peanut Butter and Banana Bites (page 72), you can scatter some granulated sugar over the human batch while keeping the dog's batch plain—though to be honest, they are good just as they are.

Chapter Four

TAKING THE BISCUITS

Meaty bones, beef casseroles, and
lamb stews are all just fine, but sometimes a dog
deserves a treat. Of course, any dog could live quite
happily and healthily on all of those, but they're not
very portable and if you start taking meaty bones
to the park, people will talk, even possibly call the
police. This chapter contains biscuits, nibbles, and
rewards that will keep you above suspicion,
and in your dog's good graces.

DOGGY BREATH BONES

- A big bunch of parsley, about 2 1/2 oz (70 g), finely chopped, stalks and leaves
- 1 large carrot, about 4 1/2 oz (130 g), grated
- 1/2 cup (60 g) grated cheddar cheese
- 2 1/3 cups (300 g) buckwheat flour or brown rice flour, plus a little more for dusting

- 5 tbsp (70 ml) olive oil
- About 3 1/2 tbsp (50 ml) hot water

REMEMBER

How much you feed your dog depends on his size, weight, and the amount of exercise he is getting. See page 16 for more details.

Makes
32
approx.

This is where this crazy adventure started. A few years ago I was working on a book about presents to make from things you grow in your garden and, being such a dog nut, I knew I had to include a recipe for dog lovers. I began making these for Barney and they've become one of my most requested recipes. Parsley contains limonene, which kills bad mouth bacteria. Thank goodness.

• ● • • • ● ● • • • ● ● ● ● ● ● • ● ● ● ● ● ● ● ● ● ● ● ● ● ● ● ● ● ●

1.   Preheat the oven to 350°F.

2.   Mix together the parsley, carrot, cheese, and flour until well combined. Trickle in the olive oil and stir in the water. Turn the mixture out onto a lightly floured surface and knead until you have a firm dough. Roll out to $\frac{1}{4}$ in (5 mm) thick and cut out with a bone-shaped cookie cutter.

3.   Lay the dough bones on baking sheets and bake in the preheated oven for 22–24 minutes, until crisp and starting to brown slightly around the edges. Cool on a wire rack.

4.   The bones will keep for a month in an airtight jar or you can freeze them for up to 4 months.

VARIATIONS

· Try making these with apple in place of the carrot—simply core the apples, then grate them with the skin on. Add a good pinch of ground cinnamon, too, if you like.
· You can use any hard cheese in this recipe—it's a great way to finish off any odds and ends left lingering in the refrigerator.

PEANUT BUTTER AND BANANA BITES

When I was testing this recipe, I left a batch on a wire rack to cool.
Our friend Lola was staying with us at the time and when I returned to
the kitchen she asked, "What are they? They are delicious!" I'm glad
that she liked them just as much as her gorgeous Staffie, Roxie.

72

- ³/₄ cup (100 g) buckwheat flour, plus a little more for dusting
- 1 generous cup (100 g) rolled oats
- 5 tbsp (70 g) salt- and Xylitol-free smooth peanut butter
- 1 small very ripe banana, mashed
- 3 tbsp ground flaxseeds
- 2 tbsp coconut oil

1. Preheat the oven to 350°F. Line a couple of baking sheets with baking parchment.

2. In a mixing bowl, stir together all the ingredients until well combined, or pulse them in a food processor. Turn the dough out onto a lightly floured surface and roll out to about ¹/₄ in (5 mm) thick. Cut into shapes using a small cookie cutter (use a bone-shaped one if you like). Place the biscuits on the prepared baking sheets. Roll out the scraps and cut into shapes, until you've used up all the dough. Bake in the preheated oven for 20 minutes, then leave to cool on the baking sheet.

3. When completely cold, store in an airtight container; they will keep for a couple of weeks, or you can freeze them for up to 4 months.

Makes
50
approx.

GRANOLA BARS

Makes
34

These are great for the pup on the go—which, let's face it, is most of them. Blackstrap molasses, used in moderation, is a good source of iron, potassium, magnesium, and B vitamins, and some believe it may help relieve the symptoms of arthritis.

- 2 ½ cups (250 g) rolled oats
- 2 ½ tbsp (20 g) pumpkin seeds
- 2 ½ tbsp (20 g) sunflower seeds
- 2 ½ tbsp (20 g) dried cranberries or blueberries
- 1 medium, ripe banana, peeled and mashed
- 1 pear, slightly unripe, cored and grated (peel on)
- 2 tbsp coconut oil
- 1 tbsp unsulphured blackstrap molasses
- A little flour, for dusting

1. Preheat the oven to 350°F. Line a couple of baking sheets with baking parchment.

2. In a food processor, pulse the oats until they form a coarse flour. Add the seeds and dried fruit and pulse again to break them up a bit. Pour into a bowl and mix in the banana, pear, coconut oil, and molasses. You want to form a stiffish dough—if it's too stiff to roll out, add a splash of water.

3. Turn the dough out onto a lightly floured surface and roll it out into a rectangle approximately ½ in (1 cm) thick. Cut the dough into bars measuring about 2 x 1 in (5 x 2.5 cm). Lay the bars onto the prepared baking sheets and bake for 22–25 minutes, until slightly golden around the edges. Leave them to firm up for 10 minutes, then place them on a rack to cool completely.

4. These will keep in a jar for a couple of weeks, or you can freeze them for up to 4 months.

LIVER BROWNIES

This is one of the few recipes in this book that is probably a dog-only dish, but boy, do they love these brownies. These make a great training treat because dogs find them irresistible.

- A little sunflower or olive oil, for greasing the tin
- 1 ¼ cups (130 g) rolled oats
- 2 ½ tbsp (25 g) dried cranberries (optional)
- 1 ²⁄₃ cups (200 g) buckwheat or brown rice flour
- 1 tsp ground cinnamon (optional)
- 9 oz (250 g) chicken, lamb, or beef liver
- 3 eggs, lightly beaten
- 2 tbsp coconut oil

Makes *Loads*

1. Preheat the oven to 350°F. Brush a 10 in (25 cm) square brownie baking pan with oil and line with baking parchment, allowing the parchment to hang over the edges of the tin because this will make the brownies easier to remove later. Brush the parchment with oil, too.

2. In a food processor, pulse the oats until they are quite fine. Add the cranberries, if using, and pulse them, too. Then add the flour and cinnamon, if using, and pulse to blend. Pour into a bowl.

3. Put the livers in the food processor with the eggs and coconut oil and pulse until fairly smooth. Add the dry mixture in three batches, pulsing until just mixed. Pour into the prepared pan and bake in the preheated oven for 30 minutes, until a toothpick inserted into the middle comes out clean. Remove from the oven and allow to cool completely in the pan, placed on a wire rack. Cut into roughly $1/2$–$3/4$ in (1–2 cm) bites.

4. The brownies will keep in a container in the refrigerator for a few days, or in the freezer for up to 4 months.

VARIATION

To make a simple liver treat, bring a pan of water to a boil, toss in some chicken livers, or chunks of beef, or lamb's liver, and simmer for 5 minutes. Drain and cut into thin slivers. Place on a baking sheet lined with baking parchment and bake at 350°F for $1/4$ hours. Turn off the heat and leave in the cooling oven until completely dried out. They will keep in the refrigerator, sealed in a container for a week, or in the freezer for 4 months You can also make these in a dehydrator (pages 78-9).

SOFT OATMEAL COOKIES

Even old dogs need treats—or perhaps especially old dogs, when you consider the back-to-back shifts of loving us and taking care of us and even on our worst days, thinking we're heroes. Hard biscuits aren't ideal for some older dogs, or for those who have had recent dental surgery and may have tender mouths.

76

- Olive oil or sunflower oil, for greasing
- 1 scant cup (7 oz) cooked butternut squash purée
- 1 tsp unsulphured blackstrap molasses
- $1/4$ tsp ground cinnamon
- $1/4$ tsp ground ginger
- $2/3$ cup (80 g) buckwheat flour or brown rice flour, plus a little more for dusting
- $1/2$ cup (50 g) rolled oats

1. Preheat the oven to 350°F. Line a baking sheet with lightly greased baking parchment.

2. Mix the squash with the molasses, cinnamon, and ginger. Stir in the flour and oats. Drop rounded teaspoons of the mixture onto the baking sheet, leaving space for them to spread out a bit. Bake in the preheated oven for 12–14 minutes, until slightly golden around the edges. Cool for 5 minutes before transferring to a wire rack to cool completely.

3. They will keep for 3–4 days in an airtight container or in the freezer for up to 4 months.

VARIATION

Use unsweetened apple sauce instead of puréed squash or pumpkin, if you like.

Makes
50

SARDINE BITES

These are so simple to make and very good—guaranteed to make your
dog run over from the other side of the park.

- 8 ½ oz (240 g) canned sardines in oil
- 2 ¼ cups (200 g) rolled oats
- ¾ cup (100 g) buckwheat flour, plus a little more for dusting
- 1 ½ tbsp unsulphured blackstrap molasses
- 1 tbsp finely chopped rosemary (optional)
- 1 ½ –3 tbsp water

1. Preheat the oven to 350°F. Line a couple of baking sheets with baking parchment.

2. Add all the ingredients except the water into a food processor and pulse together until well blended. Add just enough water to bring together into a ball—it will make quite a crumbly dough. Divide the dough in two to make it easier to handle. Roll out on a floured surface with a floured rolling pin to a thickness of ¼ in (5 mm) and cut out with a ¾ in (2 cm) round cutter, or cut into small squares with a sharp knife. Place on the prepared baking sheets and bake in the preheated oven for 25 minutes. Transfer to a wire rack to cool completely.

77

3. They will keep for a week or so in an airtight container, or freeze them for up to 4 months.

Tip

If you don't have a suitably small cookie cutter, the metal cap from a bottle of olive oil or similar bottle works perfectly well.

Using a
DEHYDRATOR

Before I started making food for my dogs, I thought dehydrators were exclusively used by health food nuts. How wrong I was. They can be bought quite cheaply, from about $40, and are incredibly useful for making dog and human food. You can use them to create all kinds of dried fruits, vegetables, and meats, which are good on their own as healthy snacks or as ingredients in more complex dishes. You can certainly make these things in the oven, but the process is much more hit or miss and the results are seldom as crisp.

Here are a few ideas to get you started. The drying time will vary depending on your dehydrator and the thickness of the pieces you put in it, so you may need to experiment at first. Use the instructions that come with your gadget as your guide.

Meat jerkys

Meat jerkys couldn't be simpler to make and your dog is guaranteed to find them delicious. Cut skinless, boneless chicken breast or lean beef into thin slices, along the grain of the meat. Lay the pieces in the dehydrator and dry for 4–12 hours, until each piece is of a uniform color and completely dried out when you cut through it.

Canned tuna

Canned tuna makes an easy treat. Simply break into big chunks and dry for 9–12 hours.

Slices of sweet potato

Slices of sweet potato make excellent, healthy chews. Slice thinly into long strips, lay in the dehydrator, and dry for 4–10 hours, until tough and leathery.

Fruit

Fruit works very well. Thin slices of apple or pear (core them first) and slices of banana take about 6–10 hours to dry out.

Gifts for your dog friends' dogs

Owning a dog can open up your life in a beautiful way.

What no one tells you is that not only do you acquire a canine companion, you often make lots of new human friends, too. When you have a dog, other dog walkers talk to you. What begins with a chat about the best leashes or where to find a great groomer can turn into some of the warmest, kindest friendships of your life. With my park posse, we've been through births, marriages, deaths, illnesses, and divorces and, at the risk of sounding all Oscar-ceremony emotional, I feel intensely fortunate to have all of my dog pals in my life.

On the first day I took Barney to the park over ten years ago, one of the regular walkers had brought homemade cake for the humans and biscuits for the dogs because it was his dog's first birthday (hello Tom, hello Polly). I thought he was crazy. Now look at me.

You may want to make one or more of the recipes in this book as a gift for one of your dog friends. It's sometimes difficult to know what to give other adults (how many scented candles does a person need?), but everyone loves a gift for their dog. Any of the biscuits or other treats in this book make great presents. Tie them in clear plastic gift bags with pretty string or ribbon, and finish it off with a bone-, dog-, or paw-shaped biscuit cutter, or seal them in brown or white paper bags with a dog-themed sticker. Print-on-demand companies can run some off for you pretty cheaply. Don't forget to label the contents of the bag!

Top Tips

KING KONGS

If you share your home with a teething puppy or a bored dog, you need to make room in your freezer for a few KONG toys. Made from tough, chewable rubber, they come in varied sizes suitable for all breeds of dog, from mini mutts to giant hounds. Their sides are angled so they bounce about erratically but, most excitingly of all, they have central cavities that you stuff with all kinds of treats. Working away to extract every last morsel will keep your dog's brain busy for ages. They are a terrific distraction if you have to leave your dog to her own devices for a few hours.

* Buy several KONGs, pack them with food and freeze them so you always have one ready when you need to go out.

* I like to stuff KONGs with a variety of foods in layers to make them as interesting and rewarding as possible. Things to include: peanut butter (ensure it does not contain salt or Xylitol), kibble, chopped cooked meat, puréed squash, mashed banana, or scraps of cheese.

* In summer, meaty stocks (page 34) or puréed fruit (pages 94-5) poured into a KONG and then frozen make a cooling treat.

* Stuffed, frozen KONGs are very soothing for teething puppies' sore gums.

* To clean a KONG, scrub out the inside as best as you can with an old toothbrush and then wash it in hot, soapy water or put it in the dishwasher. Rinse and dry well.

Brain food

While your dog might love lounging on the sofa with you or running around the park with her pals, she also loves to figure things out on her own. Keeping your dog's brain busy is a surefire way of keeping her content and, along with a good diet and plenty of exercise, can help to curb any destructive behaviors. These are games my own dogs love, and I hope yours will, too.

Turn a muffin tin upside down on the floor. Scatter some dried dog treats over the surface and let her use her paws, mouth, and nose to tease out the goodies.

Turn the muffin tin (see how useful a muffin tin can be?) the right way up. Put some treats into some of the cups and cover the cups with tennis balls. She'll have fun digging out the food.

Take a plastic water bottle and cut some random holes in the sides. Drop some treats inside and let your dog roll the bottle about to try and get them out. Never leave your dog alone with this game in case she attempts to devour the bottle, too.

Chapter Five

SPECIAL OCCASIONS

I understand that this chapter may seem for some (hi, Dad) like "A Step Too Far." Frosted cakes and frozen treats are about as far away from table scraps as you can get. But since I began writing about cooking for dogs, I've been asked to cater dog birthday parties, Christmas parties, even a dog wedding (I don't judge), so I've put some thought into creating suitably celebratory food that is still recognizably good, healthy food for happy, if pampered, hounds.

CARROT AND APPLE PUPCAKES

with cream cheese frosting

For the cakes

* A little oil, for greasing
* 1 ²/₃ cups (200 g) buckwheat flour or brown rice flour
* 1 scant cup (130 g) grated carrot
* ²/₃ cup (75 g) rolled oats

For the frosting

* 5 ¹/₂ oz (150 g) cream cheese
* scant ¹/₂ cup (90 g) unsweetened applesauce*

To decorate

* Flaxseeds, dehydrated slices of apple or carrot (page 79), finely chopped fresh rosemary (all optional)

* 1 tbsp ground flaxseeds (optional)
* 1 tsp ground cinnamon (optional)
* 1 scant cup (200 g) plain yogurt
* ²/₃ cup (150 g) unsweetened applesauce*
* 3 eggs, lightly beaten

Makes
24
mini pupcakes

These cakes are a special treat. Fruit sugars (from the apple) are still sugars, and shouldn't be consumed every day, but every now and then, it won't do any harm. Feel free to cut the cakes into even smaller pieces if you like.

1. Preheat the oven to 350°F. Lightly grease a 24-hole mini-muffin tin.

2. In a bowl, whisk together the flour, carrot, oats, flaxseeds, and cinnamon, if using. In a large glass measuring cup, whisk together the yogurt, applesauce, and eggs.

3. Gently and thoroughly mix the wet mixture into the dry mixture. Spoon into the prepared muffin tin and bake in the preheated oven for 15 minutes, until a toothpick inserted into the middle comes out clean. Cool on a wire rack.

4. When cool, prepare the frosting. In a bowl, beat together the cream cheese and applesauce until well blended—if you would like it to be super smooth, blend it in a blender or use an immersion blender.

5. Smooth the frosting over the cupcakes. Sprinkle some flaxseeds or rosemary on top to finish, or use a dehydrated apple or carrot slice if you like. Any leftovers will freeze well for 4 months.

*Either use store-bought applesauce that contains no sugar or salt, or make your own—it's very simple.

Peel, core, and chop about 3–4 (about 300 g) cooking apples and place in a pan with a good splash of water. Cook over medium heat with the lid on until the apples are cooked thoroughly and fluffy. If necessary, mash them lightly with a fork.

BEEF AND POTATO MUFFINS

These are great meaty treats—you can go to town and be super fancy if you have the time and inclination to pipe on the potato and parsley frosting.

For the muffins

- 🌸 1 tsp sunflower oil
- 🌸 1 lb 2 oz (500 g) ground beef
- 🌸 1 cup (150 g) mashed potato
- 🌸 1 egg, lightly beaten
- 🌸 1 tsp salt-free tomato paste
- 🌸 1/2 tsp freshly chopped thyme leaves

For the frosting

- 🌸 1 cup (150 g) mashed potato
- 🌸 1 heaping tbsp cream cheese
- 🌸 4–5 tbsp very finely chopped parsley, plus extra for garnishing
- 🌸 Some cooked peas, for garnishing (optional)

Makes

12

muffins or 24 mini muffins

1. Preheat the oven to 375°F. Line a 12-hole muffin tin or a 24-hole mini-muffin tin with paper liners.

2. Warm the oil in a frying pan over medium-high heat and add the beef, breaking it up with a fork and sautéing it until it has lost its pink color. Remove it from the heat and drain off the excess fat. Put the beef in a bowl and mix it together with the mashed potato, egg, tomato paste, and thyme. Spoon the mixture into the paper liners and bake in the preheated oven for 15 minutes for the small muffins, or 20 minutes for the large ones.

3. Remove the muffins from the oven and, while they are cooling, make the frosting. Mix together the potato, cream cheese, and parsley—if you want to make it a bright, vivid green, blend the mixture in a food processor or with an immersion blender. If you're being super fancy, pipe the frosting onto the cooled pupcakes, or simply spoon it on. Garnish with some more finely chopped parsley and/or with the peas.

4. Any leftovers will freeze well for 4 months.

VARIATION

These pupcakes also work very well with lamb and leftover mashed sweet potato, and seasoned with freshly chopped mint in place of the thyme.

THE DOG HOUSE'S
YAPPY BIRTHDAY CAKE

Barney and I spent a delightful weekend in southwest Wales, UK,
visiting The Dog House, an activity and education center for dogs
run by Mark and Gillian Thompson. This birthday cake is inspired by
the one they make for their VIPups, but I've gussied it up a bit with
frosting and extra biscuits. It's a special treat and a little goes a very
long way. The Thompsons say, "Candles are inadvisable, but both
human and canine singing is encouraged."

For the cake

* 2½ tbsp vegetable oil, plus a little extra for greasing the tin
* 5½ tbsp (80 g) salt- and Xylitol-free smooth peanut butter
* 5½ tbsp honey
* 1 large egg, lightly beaten
* 1 tsp vanilla extract
* 1 cup (120 g) whole-wheat flour
* ⅓ cup (50 g) grated carrot, or a combination of carrot and parsnip

For the frosting

* 6 tbsp salt- and Xylitol-free smooth peanut butter
* 3 tbsp plain yogurt

To decorate

* Some Doggy Breath Bones (page 70), made with a small cutter, or other decoratively cut dog biscuits

Makes

1

large cake

1. Preheat the oven to 350°F.

2. Lightly grease a 6½ in cake pan, line the base with baking parchment, and grease the parchment.

3. In a bowl, whisk together the oil, peanut butter, honey, egg, and vanilla. In a separate bowl, combine the flour and grated carrot. Fold the dry mixture into the wet mixture until well combined. Spoon into the prepared pan and bake in the preheated oven for 30 minutes, until a skewer inserted into the middle comes out clean. Cool for 15 minutes before turning out onto a wire rack to cool completely. Remove the paper from the cake's base.

4. When the cake has cooled completely, mix together the ingredients for the frosting and spread it over the cake. Decorate the cake with dog biscuits and serve in small, happy slices.

5. Any leftovers will freeze well for 4 months.

CHRISTMAS DINNER

- 🐾 Turkey
- 🐾 Brussels sprouts
- 🐾 Carrots
- 🐾 Parsnips
- 🐾 Peas

- 🐾 Mashed potato
- 🐾 Gravy, if not made with alcohol, or a little unsalted stock (page 34)
- 🐾 Freshly chopped parsley and/or celery leaves

Makes
1
happy pup

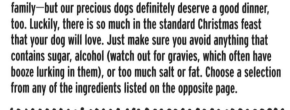

My friend Joe makes his dog salmon risotto each Christmas Day. Not all of us want to go so far—to be honest, at that time of year I'm busy enough trying to feed all of the human members of our family—but our precious dogs definitely deserve a good dinner, too. Luckily, there is so much in the standard Christmas feast that your dog will love. Just make sure you avoid anything that contains sugar, alcohol (watch out for gravies, which often have booze lurking in them), or too much salt or fat. Choose a selection from any of the ingredients listed on the opposite page.

1. Shred everything fine and moisten with gravy or stock. Serve slightly warm.

VARIATION

Shred the turkey and vegetables very fine and mix with the mashed potato and any parsley, celery leaves, thyme, or rosemary you might have. Form into patties and serve as they are, or bake them at 375°F for 20 minutes and serve slightly warm.

SUMMER PUPSICLES

Summer is a great time to be a dog owner—evening walks possibly culminating in a visit to the pub, sunny weekends in the park or on the beach and riverbank—all are great shared adventures. But dogs need special care to fully enjoy the sunshine. They can't sweat to regulate their body temperatures, so you'll need to help them keep cool in the heat. Avoid walking at the hottest time of day, particularly on boiling hot pavements, always carry water with you, and help them cool down with these great cool treats. These are a fantastic way to get your dog to eat fruit and vegetables on hot days, when proper meals can feel like too much of a chore—they're not called the "dog days of summer" for nothing. It takes minutes to whip up a batch, then either freeze in ice cube trays, small popsicle molds, or in KONG toys (page 82). Added benefit: the fruity ones are delicious for humans, too.

Good combinations

- 🐾 1 banana + 3 tbsp peanut butter (salt- and Xylitol-free) + a scant ½ cup (100 ml) unsweetened apple juice + 1 tsp ground flaxseeds

- 🐾 1¼ cups (300 g) cooked, puréed, unsweetened apple + ¾ cup (150 g) plain yogurt + pinch of ground cinnamon

- 🐾 ¾ cup (150 g) finely chopped cooked chicken + 1 generous cup (250 ml) chicken stock + 3 tbsp finely chopped fresh parsley

- 🐾 ¾ cup (200 g) puréed cucumber + ⅔ cup (100 g) peas + ⅔ cup (150 ml) chicken or vegetable stock

- 🐾 1¼ cups (300 g) puréed mango or papaya + ⅔ cup (150 ml) pineapple juice + 3 tbsp plain yogurt

CHILLY COCONUT AND STRAWBERRY BITES

Strawberries are a good source of fiber and vitamin C and they also contain malic acid, an enzyme that helps whiten teeth. Coconut oil can help improve skin and coat, aid digestion, and is beneficial for joints. Serve these outside or on a tiled floor— so much deliciousness can get messy.

🐾 1 ⅓ cups (200 g) strawberries, hulled
🐾 ¾ cup (200 g) coconut oil

VARIATION

Replace the strawberries with raspberries, which have good anti-inflammatory properties, or pineapple, which contains bromelain to aid the digestion of protein and reduce the inflammation of joints.

1. Roughly purée together the strawberries and coconut oil in a food processor, with an immersion blender, or with a potato masher. Don't overdo it, because you want some chunks of strawberry left in the mixture. Spoon into small ice cube trays and freeze, or use the mixture to stuff a KONG toy (page 82).

Sweet shortcut

If you're short on time, just remove the rind and seeds from a wedge of watermelon, cut into cubes and freeze. Absolutely chill-icious.

Makes
12–24

Chapter Six

FEEL BETTER FOOD

Even the most robust of dogs can fall prey to the occasional bout of illness, or suffer from intolerances and allergies. This chapter gives you some advice on how to begin to tackle some of these challenges, but it is very important that you consult your vet immediately should your dog have persistent or unusual symptoms.

PURÉED PUMPKIN
WITH YOGURT

Pumpkin, or squash, is a very good source of soluble fiber and vitamins A, C, and E. It's easily digestible and can help improve skin and coat problems in dogs, as well as being helpful in soothing short bouts of diarrhea and constipation. You can use canned pumpkin, too—just make sure it is plain puréed pumpkin with no added salt, sugar, sweeteners, or seasonings. Add a tablespoonful or two of this mixture to your dog's regular meal.

- A butternut squash or a big chunk of pumpkin, peeled, deseeded, and cut into chunks
- ¾ cup (200 g) plain yogurt

1. Bring a saucepan of water to a boil and add the squash or pumpkin. Simmer for about 20 minutes, until very tender when pierced with a knife. Drain in a colander and leave to steam for 10 minutes so it loses some of its excess moisture. Mash and leave to cool completely, then mix with the yogurt.

2. This will keep, covered, in the refrigerator for up to a week, or freeze it in ice cube trays (about the perfect portion size) for up to 4 months.

Makes
1
large bowl

SCRAMBLED EGGS

Eggs are easily digestible and a good source of protein as well as essential amino and fatty acids. Most dogs enjoy them even when they aren't able to eat other foods. To give the eggs an extra nutritional boost, sprinkle on a little eggshell powder (page 38), or mix them with some of the foods on the variations list (right).

- ⅟4 tsp olive oil
- 2 eggs, lightly beaten

1. Warm the oil in a small nonstick pan over medium-low heat. Add the eggs and cook, stirring, until they form soft curds. Of course, you can do this in the microwave if you want.

VARIATIONS
Mix the eggs up with some of the following:

- A little cooked brown rice
- Some mashed, canned sardines or salmon
- A little shredded, cooked meat
- A spoonful of plain yogurt or cottage cheese
- Some oatmeal (page 32)

Makes

1

bowl

FAST TALK

It's entirely normal for adult dogs to fast when they are unwell. They may do this themselves, naturally, or you may want to restrict food for 12–24 hours in response to a mild bout of sickness or diarrhea. Make sure they are comfortable and have access to plenty of fresh water, and gradually introduce small amounts of bland food, such as rice and chicken, after the initial fasting period. If you have any doubt at all about the severity of their illness—their bouts of sickness and diarrhea are frequent, there is blood in their vomit or poop, they seem listless, in pain, or just not themselves—talk to your vet immediately.

CHICKEN SOUP

Who doesn't love a delicious bowl of chicken soup when they're sick? It works very well for dogs, too—if they're really not eating much, serving it slightly warm might help because the savory smell is enticing. If you have a batch of chicken stock (page 34) in the freezer, you can make this in no time at all, but it's not a big chore to make it from scratch either. This is something I make in batches whenever I find some nice organic chicken on sale in the supermarket because it freezes really well.

- 2–3 skinless chicken breasts or legs
- 1 carrot, peeled and roughly chopped
- 1 celery rib, trimmed and roughly chopped
- 1.6 quarts (1.5 liters) water
- A selection of vegetables, chopped small, including sweet potatoes, peas, carrots, green beans, celery, zucchini, broccoli
- 1 apple, peeled, cored, and diced (optional)

FOR HUMANS

If you are serving this to humans, reserve a portion for your dog, then season what remains with salt, soy sauce, and some finely chopped chilis and spring onions.

1. Place the chicken in a saucepan with the carrot and celery and add the water. Bring to a simmer, skim off any foam that rises to the top, and cook gently for about 40 minutes until the chicken is very tender. Strain the stock into a clean saucepan and discard the vegetables.

2. When the chicken is cool enough to handle, shred it into small pieces and discard any bones, then return it to the stock pan with any remaining vegetables from the list and the apple, if using. Simmer for 20 minutes or so, until the vegetables are very tender. Cool slightly, then use a food processor or immersion blender to pulse the soup until it has a chunky, creamy consistency. Serve cold or slightly warm.

3. This will keep, covered, in the refrigerator for a couple of days or freeze in individual portions for up to 4 months.

PEARL BARLEY AND BEEF RISOTTO

Pearl barley makes a good alternative to rice for some dogs. It's easily digestible and high in fiber.

- Scant ½ cup (80 g) pearl barley
- 1 generous cup (250 ml) stock (page 34) or water
- 3½ oz (100 g) kale or cabbage, very finely shredded
- 7–14 oz (200–400 g) leftover roast beef, or other cooked beef, very finely shredded
- ⅔ cup (100 g) peas, fresh or frozen (optional)

1. Place the barley in a medium-sized saucepan with the stock or water. Bring to a boil, lower the temperature, cover, and simmer very gently until the barley is tender but still slightly chewy. This can take anywhere from 25–40 minutes, depending on the barley—check every 5 minutes or so after 25 minutes and add a little more water if necessary.

2. When the barley is almost cooked but still a little soupy, add the kale or cabbage and simmer for another 5–10 minutes until the vegetables are very tender. Add the beef and peas and warm thoroughly. Cool and serve as is, or use a food processor or immersion blender to pulse to a smooth texture.

3. This will keep, covered, in the refrigerator for a couple of days or freeze in individual portions for up to 4 months.

VARIATION

This also works really well with chicken, turkey, or lamb.

Makes
1
large pot

RICE AND CHICKEN

with parsley

- 🐾 2–3 skinless chicken breasts or thighs
- 🐾 1 quart (1 liter) water
- 🐾 ¾ cup (150 g) brown or white rice, rinsed

- 🐾 A small handful of fresh parsley leaves, finely chopped (optional)

 Tip If you're using brown rice, soak it in cold water while the chicken is cooking because this will help it cook faster.

Makes

1

large pot

Chicken and rice has long been the go-to dinner of choice for recuperating dogs. It's easy to digest and most dogs like it. White rice is bland as bland can be, and a simple source of carbs for an ill pup. Brown rice is higher in protein and nutrients and definitely worth a try if you think your dog is up to it.

• ● • • • ● • ● • • ● • • ● ● • • ● ● • ● ● ● ● ● ● • ● ● ● ● ● • ● ● ● ● ● ● ● ● • ●

1. Place the chicken in a saucepan with the water, or enough to cover. Bring to a simmer, scoop off any foam that rises to the surface, cover, and cook gently for about 40 minutes until the chicken is very tender. Scoop out the chicken pieces with a slotted spoon. When cool enough to handle, shred into small pieces and discard any bones.

2. Measure the chicken stock you have from cooking the chicken. Use this to cook the rice. Follow the instructions on the packet for cooking the rice; if you don't have enough stock, simply add more water. When the rice is cooked—you want it to be slightly softer than you would normally cook it to make it more easily digestible—spread it out on a large plate so it can cool down quickly. Mix it with the chicken and toss in the parsley if you are using it.

3. Use immediately, or freeze in individual portions for up to 4 months.

A word on allergies and intolerances

Just like people, dogs sometimes suffer from allergies—to pollen, dust, and yes, food. Food allergies can be caused by feeding our dogs the same thing day after day. Lots of commercial dog food, particularly kibble, has a high refined carbohydrate content which can irritate dogs' stomachs and sometimes lead to Adverse Food Reaction (AFR), created when our dogs continuously eat the same thing.

If you think your dog might suffer from food allergies and intolerances (see the checklist on the opposite page), first visit your vet to discuss your concerns. They will help you rule out other possible causes, such as parasitic infections like fleas or ear mites, and then discuss with you an elimination diet to try to discover if the problem is food related.

For six to twelve weeks, your dog will eat a prescribed diet—the vet may offer you a commercial brand of dog food, but try to work out together a suitable homemade one. Your dog will eat this, leaving out everything else for the trial period, then you reintroduce their previous diet for two weeks. If symptoms return, you know food was the source of the problem. Next, you put your dog back onto the elimination diet and add new ingredients gradually over a period of time, so you can detect which ingredient your dog reacts to.

There are some key differences between an allergy and an intolerance, which are important to be able to identify.

Food intolerances are the result of poor digestion. For example, lactose intolerance in humans and dogs happens when we lack or have low levels of lactase, the milk-digesting enzyme. Intolerances happen in the dog's digestive tract, as opposed to allergies, which are an immune response that can affect the dog's whole system. Many dogs find it difficult to digest cow's milk but may still be able to tolerate small amounts of cheese and yogurt (page 18) from time to time. Goat's milk in small amounts is often a more palatable alternative.

Allergies result from an over-responsiveness of the dog's immune system to certain ingredients, most commonly sources of proteins, including meat, dairy, and grains such as wheat and corn. Allergies tend to develop over time, after repeated exposure to certain ingredients. It's rare to find a dog under a year old suffering from allergies, whereas intolerances can occur at any age.

The good news is that true food allergies are rare, and the best way to prevent them is to allow your dog to experience a wide and varied delicious diet of natural foods.

105

WHAT TO LOOK OUT FOR

Signs that your dog may have developed a food allergy or intolerance may include:

- 🐾 **Excessive scratching or licking**
- 🐾 **Rashes**
- 🐾 **Runny nose**
- 🐾 **Poor coat and excessive shedding**
- 🐾 **Ear infections**
- 🐾 **Vomiting**
- 🐾 **Diarrhea**
- 🐾 **Abdominal pain**
- 🐾 **Flatulence**

Other Tricks

IS YOUR PUPPY CHEWING MORE THAN HIS DINNER?

Puppies, like human babies, explore their environment with their mouths, and they chew on hard objects to reduce the pain from incoming teeth. For older dogs, chewing on hard things is a way of keeping their jaws strong and their teeth clean. You can give them alternatives to your favorite shoes or Granny's antique armchair (see page 79), but to deter them from chewing where you'd rather they didn't, you can make sprays that are safe, easy, and cheap from ingredients you probably already have in the house.

TO MAKE A CITRUS SPRAY

This smells wonderful as well as being effective. Simmer the peels from a few oranges, lemons, or grapefruits in a pan—you want a couple of generous handfuls—with about 1 quart (1 liter) of water for 5–10 minutes, then remove from the stove and leave to cool. Strain the liquid and decant it into a spray bottle (the kind you might buy in a garden center). Spray the liquid anywhere your dog might chew (test on an inconspicuous spot first if you are going to spray fabrics). It will keep in the refrigerator for a couple of weeks.

TO MAKE A VINEGAR SPRAY

Dogs hate the smell of vinegar. You can make a simple spray by combining one part white vinegar with two parts cider vinegar in a spray bottle; use it as above. An added bonus: You can also use this spray to neutralize the odor if your dog has peed in an inappropriate place. It will deter him from relieving himself in the same spot again and the vinegar smell dissipates quite quickly so your house won't smell like the local bar at closing time.

SUPPLIERS

❀ Bob's Red Mill
To stock your pantry with organic whole-grain flours for homemade dog (or human) biscuits.
bobsredmill.com

❀ Chewy and PetSmart
Durable dog KONG toys and an assortment of slow dog bowls can be found at PetSmart stores nationwide or online.
chewy.com, petsmart.com

❀ Moo and Zazzle
For custom-printed labels and stickers for your dog gifts.
moo.com, zazzle.com

❀ NFM Directory
For local, organic produce, check out the USDA's National Farmers Market Directory.
ams.usda.gov/local-food-directories/farmersmarkets

❀ Williams Sonoma
For durable kitchen tools, including immersion blenders and baking supplies. Available online and at nearly fifty stores in North America.
williamssonoma.com

❀ Wilton
The go-to resource for cake and cookie decorators.
wilton.com

ABOUT THE AUTHOR

Debora Robertson is a food, gardening, and lifestyle writer and editor. She was associate food editor of *Red* magazine and Hugh Fearnley Whittingstall's food editor at River Cottage. She has written for a wide variety of publications, including *The Guardian*, the *Daily Telegraph*, *The Sunday Telegraph*, *The Times*, the *Daily Mail*, *The Independent on Sunday*, *Waitrose Food Illustrated*, *Waitrose Kitchen*, *Country Life*, *Country Living*, and *Sainsbury's Magazine*. She writes frequently for the *Daily Telegraph* on modern manners and all domestic matters. She lives in East London with her husband, Séan, her dogs, Barney and Gracie, and her very patient cat, Dixie.

ACKNOWLEDGMENTS

This book began with a piece I wrote for the *Daily Telegraph,* commissioned by food editor Amy Bryant, on the slightly embarrassing joy I derive from cooking for my dogs. This inspired further pieces, commissioned by Celia Duncan at the *Daily Mail* and Paula Lester at *Country Life.* I thank them all for their enthusiasm, and for allowing me to write about my love of cooking and my love of dogs. Also, many thanks to Samantha Harvey, for not thinking I was crazy to suggest dogs' dinners cooking classes at Divertimenti.

Katie Cowan at Pavilion Books saw one of these pieces and sent me a tweet to ask if I might think of turning the idea into a book. We arranged a meeting and I brought in some Doggy Breath Bones for her border terrier, Rooney. He was also at the meeting and ate them with great enthusiasm, so I owe him a debt of gratitude, too—a bit of a nail biter there for a minute. It has been a delight to work with all of the Pavilion gang. Thank you Katie, Caitlin Leydon, Michelle Mac, Helen Lewis, and Polly Powell for being so brilliant, kind, and patient. I can't begin to tell you how grateful I am to Cinzia Zenocchini for her rich, enchanting illustrations.

A huge thanks always and forever to the wonderful Julia Platt Leonard, for helping me with recipe testing and for always saying, "Yes, why not?" And to her dogs, Olivia and Boyare, for their enduring enthusiasm for leftovers. Thank you to The Dog House for allowing me to include their birthday cake recipe. Thanks, too, to my Clissold Park dog-walking posse, including Mark and Nico and Lexie, Sarah and Wilma and Lola, Tom and Polly, Gez and Baxter, Chris and Duffy, Lola and Roxie, for all of the early morning wit, wisdom, and coffee. And to Kris Collins, for cheerfully taking the leashes and walking my dogs when I am not able to.

I am indebted to Louise Glazebrook, of thedarlingdogcompany.co.uk, for generously sharing her insights into dogs and humans with me over the years.

Thanks to Caroline Michel and Tessa David at Peters Fraser & Dunlop, for excellent advice and tireless agenting.

The hugest of thank-yous to Séan Donnellan for everything, always, but in this instance for saying, "Yes, all right then," and giving me Barney.

But most of all, eternal gratitude and endless love to Barney and Gracie, always good dogs.

INDEX